STUNTS, TRICKS, AND JUMPS

MOTORCYCLE MANIA

David and Patricia Armentrout

Rourke
Publishing LLC
Vero Beach, Florida 32964

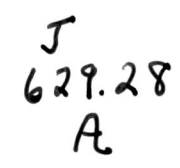

© 2008 Rourke Publishing LLC

All rights reserved. No part of this book may be reproduced or utilized in any form or by any means, electronic or mechanical including photocopying, recording, or by any information storage and retrieval system without permission in writing from the publisher.

www.rourkepublishing.com

PHOTO CREDITS: Cover and pp. 5 ©Alistair Cotton; title page, pp. 4, 7, 12, 14 © keith robinson; pp. 6, 22 © Honda Media; pp. 8 ©Michael Stokes; pp. 9 ©Stephen Coburn; pp. 10, 13 ©Anson Hung; pp. 15 ©Steve Bruhn; pp. 16 ©Jae C. Hong; pp. 16, 19, 21 ©Associated Press; pp. 17 ©BMW; pp. 19 ©Gautam Singh.

Title page: *A good motocross course has jumps, dips, and curves.*

Editor: Robert Stengard-Olliges

Cover design by Nicola Stratford

Library of Congress Cataloging-in-Publication Data

Armentrout, David, 1962-
  Stunts, tricks, and jumps / David and Patricia Armentrout.
    p. cm. -- (Motorcycle mania II)
  ISBN-13: 978-1-60044-591-0
  1. Motorcycles--Juvenile literature. I. Armentrout, Patricia, 1960- II. Title.
  TL440.15.A766 2008
  629.28'475--dc22
                                    2007016380

Printed in the USA

CG/CG

Rourke Publishing

www.rourkepublishing.com – rourke@rourkepublishing.com
Post Office Box 3328, Vero Beach, FL 32964

TABLE OF CONTENTS

Stunts, Tricks, and Jumps 4

FMX 6

Big Air 8

Freestyle 12

Tricks and Jumps 14

Stunts 16

Motorcycle Daredevil 20

Experts Only 22

Glossary 23

Index/Further Reading 24

STUNTS, TRICKS, AND JUMPS

Most people naturally try to avoid danger. Children are taught from an early age to be careful. But some people never learn that lesson. A few even search out danger.

At first glance, riders who perform motorcycle **stunts** may appear to be taking extreme risks. Their tricks are dangerous, but the best riders are skilled athletes. Their death defying tricks are well planned and practiced.

Some maneuvers are best left to the experts.

A rider dismounts his bike in mid-air.

FMX

Motocross racing takes riders over rough, off road **terrain** with steep jumps and bumps. The first racer across the finish line wins.

Freestyle Motocross (FMX) is a competition of skill, style, and nerve rather than speed. Riders are judged on their ability to perform **aerial** tricks and maneuvers.

A rider uses the bike's weight and momentum to his advantage.

Young riders learn the ups and downs of motocross.

FMX competitors ride modified motocross motorcycles. These high performance bikes are lightweight and powerful.

BIG AIR

FMX riders compete in two main events, *Big Air* (or *Best Trick*) and *Freestyle Motocross*.

Big Air is a fan favorite. Riders get three chances to show off their best trick. They begin by launching themselves and their motorcycle off a ramp at high speed. While airborne, they perform breathtaking tricks with their bikes before coming in for a landing on another ramp. Judges score the riders based on trick difficulty and overall performance.

Landings are often the toughest part of a trick.

A rider pulls off the Cliffhanger trick.

Big Air riders use specially designed ramps. Many **elite** riders build their own ramps for practice.

Competition ramps are about eight feet (2.43 meters) tall and can rocket riders more than 30 feet (9.14 meters) into the air. Riders may remain airborne for 100 feet (30.48 meters) or more.

A rider must maintain control of the bike at all times.

A large crowd watches as a trick rider gets huge air between ramps.

FREESTYLE

During *Freestyle Motocross* events, riders tackle courses full of steep, heart stopping jumps. Riders develop routines that include plenty of tricks and jumps. Judges give points for originality, difficulty, and overall performance. The rider with the highest score wins.

Attempting the Kiss of Death trick.

To pull off extreme tricks, riders must remain airborne as long as possible.

TRICKS AND JUMPS

Freestyle is all about tricks and jumps. Harder tricks score favor with fans, and points with judges.

Tricks once thought to be nearly impossible are now expected. Riders pull off radical tricks such as the Heel Clicker, Cliffhanger, Superman Seat Grab, and Kiss of Death. Innovative riders like Travis Pastrana, Nate Adams, and Brian Deegan introduce incredible new tricks year after year.

A rider nails the Superman Seat Grab.

Travis Pastrana executes a flawless back flip.

At the 2006 X Games, Travis Pastrana landed the first ever double back flip, and yes, he won the event.

STUNTS

Professional and amateur stunt men and women perform amazing, and in some cases, meaningless, feats. However, their motorcycle stunts always draw a crowd. Riders don't create stunts to compete against other riders; they perform high flying, jaw dropping performances for movies, television shows, and live audiences.

Mike Metzger flips over the fountains at Caesars Palace in Las Vegas.

Tricks require balance and focus.

Some stunt riders jump over cars, trucks, busses, and even trains trying to break world records. Others ride through rings of fire, over cliffs, and jump from one building to another to impress their audience. The stunts are very dangerous, but motorcycle stunt riders know their abilities and understand the limits of their machines.

Motorcycle stunts don't always end well. Many riders break bones and suffer long lasting injuries in failed stunt attempts.

A stuntman rockets through a ring of fire.

MOTORCYCLE DAREDEVIL

Motorcycle **daredevil** Evel Knievel became famous for jumping over rattlesnake pits, mountain lions, and a tank full of sharks. He even attempted a jump over the Snake River Canyon in a rocket powered "skycycle." The attempt came up a little short when his braking parachute deployed early. Fortunately, he landed safely after the skycycle drifted down into the canyon.

Evel Knievel prepares to jump his skycycle over Snake River Canyon.

EXPERTS ONLY

Motorcycle stunts, tricks and jumps are fascinating to watch, but can be dangerous to perform. Tricks should never be attempted without proper training. New riders should learn safety techniques from qualified instructors.

An instructor discusses the importance of safety with a group of new riders.

GLOSSARY

aerial (AIR ee ul) — happening in the air

daredevil (DAIR dev il) — someone who takes risks and does dangerous things

elite (ih LEET) — a group of people considered to be the best in a particular category

motocross (MOE toe kross) — cross-country motorcycle racing

stunts (STUHNTS) — acts that show daring and great skills

terrain (tuh RAYN) — ground, or land

INDEX

Adams, Nate   14
Cliffhanger   9
Deegan, Brian   14
FMX   6, 7, 8
Freestyle Motocross   8, 12
Heel Clicker   14
Kiss of Death   12, 14
ramp   8, 10
skycycle   20
stunts   4, 16, 18, 22
Superman Seat Grab   14
tricks   4, 6, 8, 12, 14, 22
Pastrana, Travis   14, 15

FURTHER READING

Levy, Janet. *Freestyle Motocross*. Rosen Publishing Group, 2007.
Schwartz, Tina. *Motocross Freestyle*. Capstone Press, 2004.
Sievert, Terri. *Travis Pastrana: Motocross Legend*. Capstone Press, 2005.

WEBSITES TO VISIT

expn.go.com
www.fmx.cc.com
www.fmxriders.com

ABOUT THE AUTHORS

David and Patricia Armentrout specialize in writing nonfiction books for young readers. They have had several books published for primary school reading. The ^   trouts live in Cincinnati, Ohio, with their two children.